the refugee
and the little lost
Kitten

words by: anuna nina art by: abz hakim

"For Baba, who taught me 123
and for Ron, who loved my stories"

For the child who dreams of
living a better day,
Longing to roam their town
safely and play.

For the family who wishes
for life without danger,
And the village living in fear
of the uniformed stranger.

For you all, I wish safety,
freedom and peace,
May you return to your homes
and no longer need to flee.

May your lands know freedom
and your hearts feel joy,
For you is this story of a little
refugee boy.

One night a little boy lay in bed counting sheep,
He heard an odd noise, but everyone was asleep.

He built up some courage and then went about looking,
To see what mischief could possibly be cooking.

He ventured outside, but saw nothing there,
'That's odd,' he thought, "Could it have been a bear?"

Back in the house he went, and looked up and down,
In all of the bedrooms, nothing was to be found!

He looked in the living room, even under the drapes,
'No one seems to be here, there's not a hair out of place!'

Walking past the kitchen, he heard sound from the cupboard,
'But it's full of dry food, shall I look anyway?' He wondered.

He took out the boxes - rice, cereals and crackers...
...then right at the back he heard the pitter-patters!

A tiny, little kitten sat looking lost and scared!
For a moment the two of them just sat and stared.

He saw the little kitten was very afraid,
'Hi... I was just enquiring about the noise you made.

What are you doing hiding away in the dark?'
'I can't find Mum! We got separated at the park.'

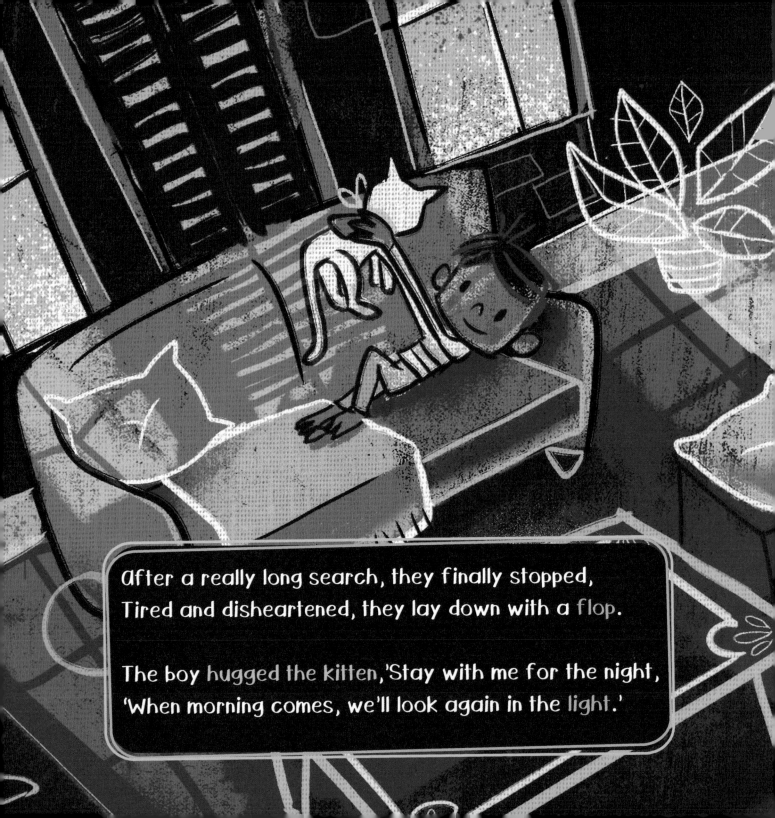

After a really long search, they finally stopped,
Tired and disheartened, they lay down with a flop.

The boy hugged the kitten, 'Stay with me for the night,
'When morning comes, we'll look again in the light.'

But then just as the two were falling asleep,
The boy heard a noise and sat up for a peep.

He crept to the window and what did he see?
Mummy cat with her paws, knocking desperately!

The boy looked over at the little lost cat,
And thought of when he too, had been lost just like that...

The war in his country meant he'd had to flee,
Far away from home, he was now a refugee.

The boy crawled over and woke up his new friend,
He loved him already and didn't want their time to end.

'I hoped we could be friends forever you see,

As you appeared to be a little refugee just like me!'

The kitten leaned in and gave the little boy a kiss.
'We will come back and visit but for now keep this.'

Mummy cat gifted her baby's blue ribbon,
'Thank you so much for finding my little lost kitten!'

the author
anuna nina

Hello!

LOVES: tea, yoga & travel

Anuna Nina is a secondary school English teacher working in London. Her mother came to the UK as a refugee, so the displacement of people fleeing war across the world is a cause she cares deeply about. Having previously worked in refugee camps from Calais to The West Bank in Palestine, she is passionate about bringing awareness to the plight and experiences of refugees.

When she's not in the classroom laughing along with her students, you can find her at the park, balancing

Abz Hakim is a published Jordanian-Canadian graphic designer and illustrator who has worked with a wide range of clients on various projects ranging from kids books, to logos, animated games and much more! His true passion remains working on kids book illustrations, designing characters, portraits and abstract paintings in his studio.

When Abz isn't creating art, you can expect him to be backpacking the world somewhere, taking photos and exploring food markets and playing with any cat he may find along his way!

Words Definitions:

FLEE To run away from something in fear

REFUGEE Someone who has fled their home and is seeking safety in another country

REFUGEE CAMP A place where refugees live whilst waiting to be placed in a safe country

BABA Arabic word for father

DISHEARTENED To feel like you've lost hope and energy

Refugee Facts:

51% of refugees are children.

The largest refugee camp in the Middle East is Za'atari refugee camp in Syria.

There are 35 million refugees in the world today and most of them come from Syria (6.6 million).

3 million of them now live in Turkey.

Help the little kitten find its way to mummy cat!

help me find my mummy ♥

Start

end

" There is only One race...
the human race.

There is only One religion...
humanity."

"Always be a little kinder than necessary."

Printed in Great Britain
by Amazon

40895434R00016